Bees and Honey

By Oxford Scientific Films

Photographs by David Thompson

G. P. Putnam's Sons   New York

First American Edition 1977
Text Copyright © 1976 by Nature's Way/G. Whizzard Publications Ltd.
Photographs © 1976 by Oxford Scientific Films Ltd.
All rights reserved.
Printed by Toppan Printing Co. Singapore

Library of Congress Cataloging in Publication Data
Main entry on title: Bees and honey.
SUMMARY: Text and photographs introduce the
inhabitants of and activities within a beehive.
1. Bees—Juvenile literature. [1. Bees]
I. Thompson, David. II. Oxford Scientific Films.
QL568.A6B38 1977   595.7'99   76-45849
ISBN 0-399-20589-6   ISBN 0-399-61078-2 lib. bdg.

Bees and Honey

The Hive

More and more, honeybees live in domesticated hives, bred under controlled conditions. Wild colonies can still be found, however, in hollow trees and in the cavities of rock-faces, walls, and so on. Ideally, the nesting-place should be dry, draft-proof, free from other occupants, and about a third of a cubic meter (about a third of a cubic yard) in size. Beekeepers have developed various types of hive to fulfil these requirements, and to ease the task of handling the inmates.

Inside the hive, the bees build ranks of combs — each comb being a vertical sheet of wax with rows of horizontally arranged cells on either side. The cells are hexagonal in shape. They are used for storing honey and pollen, and as breeding compartments for new bees. Most cells are about 0.5 cm (1/5 inch) in diameter and 1.2 cm (1/2 inch) in depth. The wax is secreted in tiny strips from glands on the underside of the worker bee's stomach. The bee moulds it into shape with its jaws.

Whether wild or domesticated, the honeybee colony has the same rigid caste system, which is the key to its organization and efficiency. There are three categories of bee: Queen, Drone and Worker.

The Queen

The queen, who is about 2 cm (3/4 inch) long, is the largest of the trio. There is normally only one to each colony, and her main role is to lay eggs — up to 200,000 a year. She is fed by the workers and, once mated, never leaves the hive, except to lead a swarm. In addition to her vital reproductive function, the queen provides the main cohesive force of the colony by producing a scent known as 'queen substance', which keeps the workers active and under control. Without it, they become lax and restless, and the colony loses its vitality and direction. Each queen has her own individual scent, which is the trademark of the hive. When the queen becomes old and exhausted, and her laying rate drops, the workers start rearing her replacement.

The queen grows from a fertilized egg. Within the first two weeks of her adult life, she is mated—often several times, and always outside the hive. This provides the queen with sufficient sperm for at least three years egg-laying. The length of a queen's life varies, but many survive for as long as four years.

The Worker

The workers are infertile females developed, like the queen bee, from fertilized eggs. The adult worker performs many duties, carrying out most, if not all, of the following tasks: feeding larvae; building and cleaning cells; regulating the hive temperature; defending the colony; foraging for water, nectar and pollen; converting nectar into honey.

A worker bee lives for about five weeks if hatched in summer; six or more months if hatched in autumn (hibernating until the spring). A strong colony may have as many as 40,000.

The Drone

Drones are fertile males, produced from unfertilized eggs. Unlike the worker or queen, they have no sting, and contribute nothing to the daily running of the colony. Their principal function is to fertilize virgin queens. Drones live for about four weeks only, and towards autumn, or when food is short, they are evicted by the workers and left to perish.

Breeding

The fertilized queen begins laying her eggs in early spring and carries on through to late autumn. She lays a maximum of 1500 a day: roughly one egg every minute. By controlling the release of the sperm stored inside her, the queen is the determining factor as to whether or not an egg is fertilized and — thus the sex of the bee. Eggs for drones (unfertilized and male) are laid in slightly larger cells than those for workers (fertilized and female); while those for queen bees are deposited in the largest cells of all. This means that although it is the queen who fertilizes the eggs, the worker bees play their part by constructing the size of the cells according to the needs of the hive.

The queen lays each egg in a clean, empty cell. After about four days, the egg hatches into a small larva, and is immediately fed by workers — or 'nurse-bees' as they are called when carrying out this particular function. Food consists of honey, pollen, and a nutritious milky substance, produced by glands in the nurse-bee's mouth.

The larval stage lasts five days. At the end of that time, the workers cap each breeding cell with a wax lid. During the next twelve days or so, the transition from larva to pupa to bee takes place in the enclosed cell.

When ready to emerge, the young adult bee bites through the cell cap and crawls out on to the comb-face. If it's a worker, the busy life starts at once. For the first three weeks of her brief existence, she will carry out in-hive activities; her last two weeks are spent as a forager.

Foraging

Workers freely exchange food and water: a bee with a surplus readily supplying other bees. The hive requirements are communicated to the foragers by means of a simple supply-and-demand mechanism. If the hive needs water for cooling, foragers bringing in water will be enthusiastically received by the home-bees; those with nectar will be made less welcome. Foragers are thus encouraged to collect water. If the demand is for nectar, the emphasis is reversed, and so on.

Before entering upon their final two weeks of

foraging, workers spend a number of days on guard duty at the hive entrance. From there they will make short flights to investigate intruders and, if necessary, attack. They also take the opportunity of familiarizing themselves with the local surroundings.

Bees and many flowering plants have evolved together. The plants have developed flower patterns and colors that are attractive to bees, and provide them with nectar and pollen; while the bees, in the process of collecting, perform the vital function of cross-pollination. In short, they help each other out.

Nectar is carried by the worker in a special compartment in its stomach. On returning to the hive, the bee regurgitates the nectar, handing it over to other workers who convert it, via their own stomachs, into honey. This takes just a few hours. The honey is then stored in cells as food. Pollen is collected on the bee's furry body and in sacs—pollen baskets—on its hind legs. Like the honey, it is kept in cells until needed.

The Dance

If a worker finds a source of food, she communicates the information to her fellow bees through an elaborate 'dance-language'. The pattern and rhythm of the dance accurately describe the location of the source: this enables the colony's efforts to be concentrated on the most profitable areas. There are two types of dance: the Round Dance and the Waggle Dance. Both are performed on the comb-face, inside the hive.

The Round Dance — quick, circular movements, first in one direction, then the other — means that food is within a radius of 100 meters (about 110 yards) or so. In other words, close to the hive.

The Waggle Dance — a figure-eight with a long, straight line separating the two loops — indicates that the source is farther afield. The sun's position is used as a 'marker' in pointing out the direction. The angle between the vertical on the comb-face and the straight line of the dance is the same as that between the sun and the food source, as seen from the hive entrance. If, for example, the two coincide, it means that the food is towards the sun.

The bee waggles its body when travelling along the straight line — hence the name of the dance. The distance from hive to food source is shown by the number of complete figure-eights traced per minute. As with the Round Dance, the type of flower is indicated by the scent carried on the returning bee's body. In performing the dance, the bee makes allowances for cross-winds, head and tail winds, etc. The margin of error is less than five per cent.

Swarming

If a colony becomes over-crowded and all the cells full, the workers are forced into idleness. The colony reacts by swarming. Two weeks before a swarm

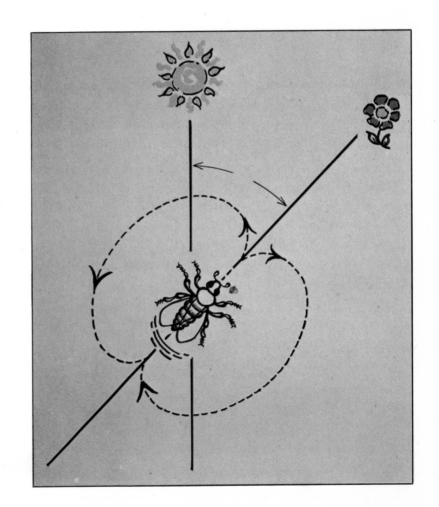

leaves, workers prepare a number of queen cells, in each of which the resident queen lays a fertilized egg. Out of one of these will come her successor, some fifteen days later.

The old queen leaves the colony accompanied by most of the foraging workers, who, before departing, take in as much honey as their honey-stomachs will hold. The swarm settles in a nearby tree, while scouts search for a suitable new home. The dance-language is used as a means of 'comparing notes'. The swarm may have to last for several days, even weeks, living off their reserves, before the scouts agree on somewhere.

Meanwhile, in the parent hive, the virgin queens are about to emerge. One of two things now happens: either the first one out destroys all the other queen cells and their occupants; or the young queens fight it out to the death — leaving just one survivor. She is mated within two weeks, and becomes the new queen of the colony.

A colony of honeybees can have as many as 60,000 individuals, most of them workers. In a good year they can produce something like 60 kilos (132½ pounds) of honey. Half is eaten by the bees themselves during the summer when the hive is active; the rest is stored for the winter hibernation. In the case of domestic hives, the latter is harvested by the beekeeper for human consumption and is replaced with quantities of sugar so that the bees can survive. In some parts of the world, such as Australia and North America, the annual yield of honey from a single hive can be as high as 300 kilos (661½ pounds).

Altogether, there are more than 20,000 different species of bee in the world — but few can match the life-style and industry of the remarkable honey-bee.

The photographs you are about to see show the bee in its environment magnified many, many times by use of special cameras and techniques.

The Honeybee lives in wild colonies or domesticated hives like this one.

The comb inside the hive is made of wax produced by the worker bee.

The Queen, who is the largest of the three bees, rules the colony.

The Drone's main job is to fertilize the Queen.

The Worker does practically everything else in the hive.

The Queen lays each egg in a separate cell. (A yellow spot put there by the beekeeper identifies the Queen.)

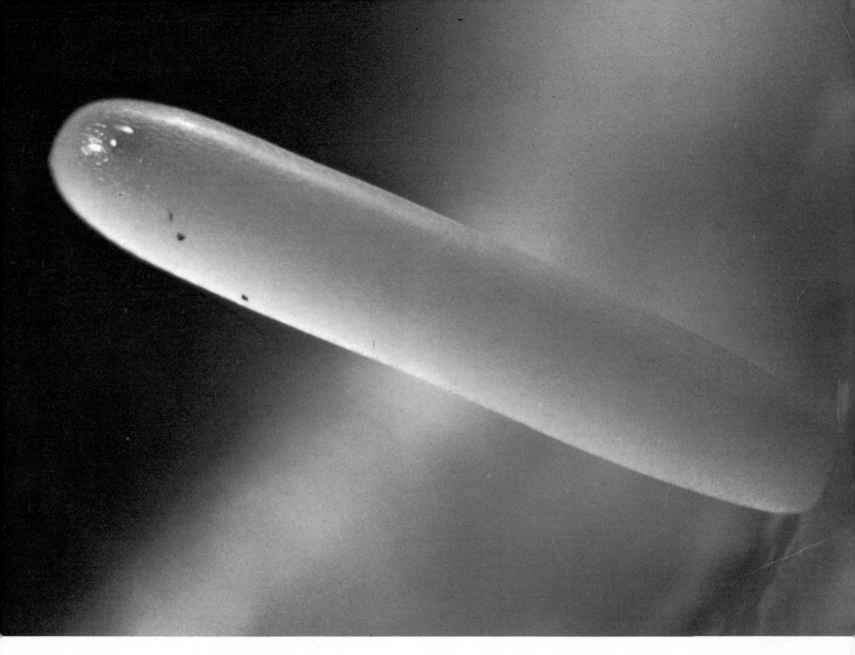

In season, she lays one egg about every minute. This is one of them.

 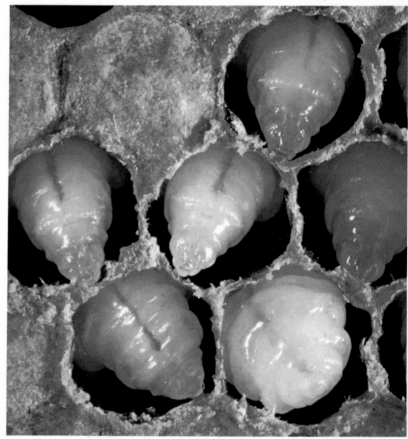

After four days the eggs hatch into larvae – five days later they are fully grown.

Some workers act as 'nurse bees' and feed the larvae.

Each cell is then capped with a wax lid. The change from larva to pupa to bee takes place inside.

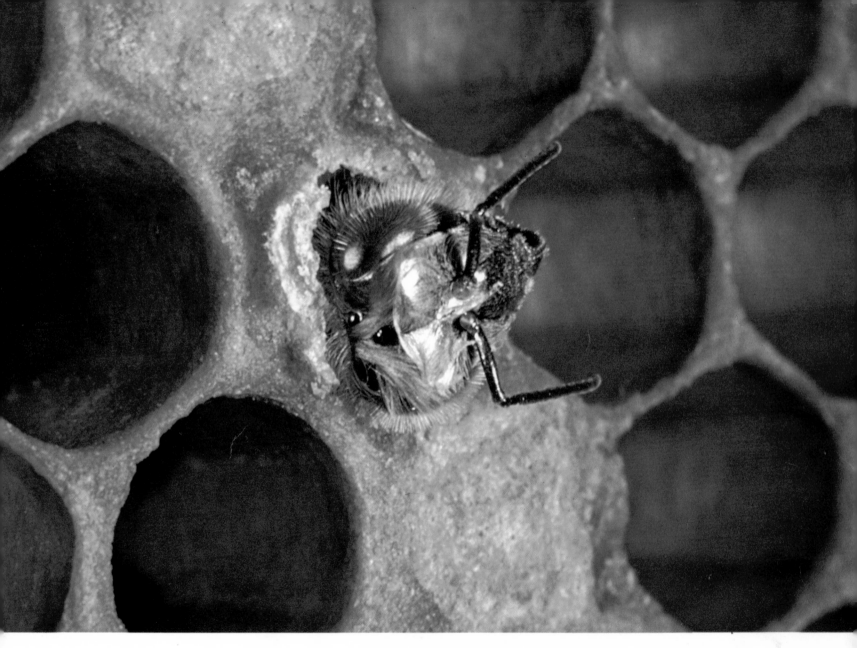

When ready, the young bee bites through the cell cap and crawls out.

Workers build and look after the comb face . . .

and supply food for the colony.

They also guard the hive against intruders . . .

and collect nectar and pollen from the flowers.

They carry nectar in their stomachs and pollen in 'baskets' on their hind legs.

They convert the nectar into honey – which, like pollen,
is stored in cells.

Bees pass on information about food sources through a special 'dance language' – this is the Round Dance.

When the old hive becomes too crowded, some bees leave to set up a new one – swarming in a nearby tree until they find a suitable place.